THE CODE

THE CODE

HOW TO WIN IN THE GAME OF LIFE AND BUSINESS.

Greg Gathers

ISBN: 1544749015
ISBN 13: 9781544749013

This book is dedicated to Maura, my wife and best friend, who inspires me every day to be better than I was the day before. Your encouragement, faith, and perspective has changed my reality.

Arabella, Alex, Paityn, Audrey, Keaton, and Hayley. You are the driving force behind every decision I make. Thank you for keeping me on my toes.

INTRODUCTION

One of the greatest achievements known to humankind is success in business. You don't have to be a gifted athlete, a cover model, or a phenomenal singer to achieve it. You also don't have to be born into it to be very successful. I was none of those things. Among my immediate family members, I am the first entrepreneur—the first to go against the grain and dismiss the advice of "Go to school, get a job, work for someone else, work hard, and save." I did have a few jobs while in school, and I did graduate from Kansas State University in 2001. I did work hard—very hard. And I did save a little—very little.

I didn't set out to grow a big business; I was just drawn to the satisfaction and pride I got from being the one who was in charge of achieving results. And I liked what I was doing. Let me rephrase that: I loved what I was doing. And I still do. *Passion* for your work is one of the most important things you must have to be successful in business. It takes an incredible amount of hard work and long hours to start and build a business. Most entrepreneurs wouldn't want to count the hours they have put into building their businesses. If they did, they might realize that they could have probably made more working for minimum wage for the same hours. But to think like that would be extremely narrow minded. Entrepreneurs must be big thinkers and see the big picture. You must think of what you are building for the future. Small thinkers reap small rewards and do small things. Big thinkers reap big rewards and do big things. That doesn't mean big thinkers are better people; they just think differently.

I suppose my entrepreneurial career started in 1995. I began selling firewood while still in high school, and I continued to sell it through college. I would cut, split, and stockpile wood year round to prepare. Then I would take out a classified ad in the winter months and deliver the wood when calls came in. Besides requiring a lot of tough manual labor, it taught me how to sell and how to differentiate myself from the competition. I learned how important results were. If I didn't sell that load of wood and deliver it, I didn't get paid. I wasn't on a time clock anymore. It also taught me how to interact with customers and their demands, although I didn't realize it at the time.

I began my tree-and-lawn service in 1999, knowing almost nothing about the industry. I advertised for mowing, landscaping, tree-and-shrub trimming or removal, and yard cleanup. I owned very little equipment and even borrowed a friend's trailer to haul tree limbs. I kept at it and learned as I went, and the company evolved into providing only tree-trimming-and-removal services. Through the years, I was able to add equipment and personnel. We experienced good growth year after year.

A few things changed in 2005 that ultimately added to the services we offered and opened my eyes to a new opportunity. A storm named Katrina slammed into the Gulf Coast on August 29, 2005. I received a call from a competitor wanting to know if I would send a crew to Louisiana to help with the cleanup. We stocked up on supplies, not really knowing what we were in for, and headed south.

The devastation was incredible and so widespread that it seemed as though there would be work forever. What Katrina showed me was that there was more to the tree business than just residential work.

I was used to small companies back home making maybe $1,000 to $2,000 a day. Now we were working on multimillion-dollar jobs for entire cities and counties with several hundred crews. I was fascinated not only by the sheer size of the jobs but also by how they were managed by the prime contractors. I decided then that I wanted to grow the business into providing contracting services to governments in addition to residences. This also led me to an important turning point for the tree service and my career. I began to work *on* the business instead of *in* the business, which allowed it to grow.

And grow it did. From 2006 to 2008, we had a three-year sales growth of 809 percent—from $200,000 to more than $2,000,000 in gross revenue! That was good enough to land us at number 286 on the Inc. 500 list for 2009. We were also honored as the 2009 Existing Small Business of the Year by the Kansas Small Business Development Center in our region. Things were going great. I started another business rehabbing houses and flipping or renting them out. I was on a roll and thought I couldn't lose.

Well, I did lose. In 2009, after a major ice storm in Kentucky, I lost a substantial amount of money on a contract we worked on. Also in 2009 and 2010, partly due to economic conditions, our residential sales dropped, and we didn't have any large contracts as we had in 2008. It left me in a deep financial hole by the end of 2010. I considered bankruptcy for a moment, which so many other companies went ahead with. But I was not going to give up and let that happen. I still feel the sting and impacts of that loss, but it was a valuable lesson learned. I'm a tenacious person, and I'm glad I didn't give up. I became more determined than ever to achieve my goal. I increased my activity level and was committed to do whatever it took to push the business forward. *Perseverance* is a key quality for an entrepreneur.

I never had a formal business education or a business mentor. Much of what I learned came from seeing what worked for other successful people. I would then apply it to my own situation. I also learned many things the hard way. Unfortunately, those things usually cost the most.

This short book is the compilation of more than five years' worth of notes and sayings scribbled on countless pieces of paper. It contains valuable tips that will help you win in the game of business. The title of each chapter is a statement that I expand on briefly which you can apply to your own business or, in many cases, your life in general. A chapter is meant to get you thinking about its topic. It is not an all-inclusive survey of the topic. A person could probably write an entire book about each topic. Some of the advice includes my own personal opinions, which you may or may not agree with, and that's okay. Take what works for you and run with it. There are no set-in-stone rules. Most entrepreneurs go against the grain and make their own rules. The advice in this book is clear and concise, and it's from real-life situations. *Time is the most important thing on this earth,* and I don't like to waste yours any more than I like wasting mine. These tips have helped me in growing my business from nothing to achieving a certain level of success and making a comeback after near defeat. My game is far from over, and I have much yet to learn and do. I challenge you to do the same. My name is Greg Gathers, and I am proud to be in the game of business. I hope you find this book useful as well as enjoyable to read.

CHAPTER 1

THE CODE

What is The Code? It sounds like a dark, mysterious secret that only a few privileged souls will ever know. Nothing could be further from the truth—The Code couldn't be simpler. It is a standard that you should hold yourself to. It's a belief that you should live by. *The Code is this: always try to be better than you were the day before in whatever it is that you do.* Always improve. Strive to be better in your career, your relationships, and your health. Every day of my life, I try to be a better business owner, a better husband, a better father, and a better person. I try to have better health, physically as well as mentally. I work for better financial health for my company and my family. I don't always achieve these things. I often fail at them and may even go backwards. The Code doesn't say you will achieve success just because you try to or say you will. You must be committed to The Code. You must believe it and follow it even when the going is tough. You don't fail if you suffer setbacks; you fail only if you settle for giving less than your all. That is ultimate failure. Go all in, never settle, and never say, "That's good enough."

Life is dynamic and moving. To be the best and stay on top, you must always be trying to better yourself. The speed of business is fast; it hardly ever slows down, and it never stops. It's the world we live in. You must constantly be striving to stay ahead of the curve. If you relax and become complacent, you will eventually be passed by someone who stayed the course. Be obsessive about success and winning and what you can do to get yourself one step closer to ultimately achieving your goals. Live by The Code.

CHAPTER 2

MANAGE PROBLEMS

The Code doesn't say you won't have problems. The only way not to have problems is to be dead. Everyone has problems, and you will have more than you think you should and more than you have planned on. The key is not to dwell on the problems. I have problems. I get upset, I get depressed, and I get negative. There are days I wonder what the hell I am doing and I want to quit. But I don't stay in that mind-set very long. Focusing on a problem won't solve it, and it sure won't move me closer to my goals. I've been an entrepreneur for more than seventeen years now, and there have been countless problems. Some of which I can't even remember. Problems are opportunities to shine. You can't move forward by focusing on a problem and being overwhelmed by it. Focus on finding a solution and the opportunity that the problem is creating. Change your focus, and change your life.

CHAPTER 3

DON'T JUST DO SOMETHING FOR A PERSON; TEACH THE PERSON HOW TO DO IT HIMSELF OR HERSELF

I remember a saying from church when I was a kid: "Give a man a fish, and you will feed him for a day; teach a man to fish, and he will never go hungry." The same can be applied to the business world. If you are always doing a task for someone else, you are wasting time for both of you. But if you show that person how to do the task, then he or she can perform it alone. This allows you to focus on more productive tasks and be more efficient. Furthermore, that person can then teach others how to perform the same task.

CHAPTER 4

BE A TOUGH NEGOTIATOR

The best deals are when both sides win. Both parties should feel as if they are getting at least something they want. I'm not saying you should give in foolishly, but a positive experience in negotiating anything should leave the door open to future business that could mean a lot of money down the road. Know everything there is to possibly know about the deal beforehand, and understand what the other side wants. Put yourself in the other person's shoes and see the issue from his or her perspective. You might be surprised.

Know what you want, have a backbone, do your homework, and don't be afraid to walk away if the deal doesn't work for you. There is nothing wrong with walking away if it's not right. In the future, the same deal, or maybe even a better one, may come together.

Be a tough negotiator, and carry a big chainsaw.

CHAPTER 5

THERE IS ALWAYS A WAY; JUST LOOK FOR IT

Can't is a bad word that should be permanently stricken from your vocabulary. There is almost always more than one way to do something; you just must see it. Often people focus on the problem instead of the solution. If at first a solution isn't apparent, step back for a minute and try to think of all the possible outcomes and the positive and negative impacts. Have a brainstorming session by yourself, or ask a trusted coworker to join. The more brains you have working, the more possible solutions you will come up with. Be solution oriented.

CHAPTER 6

DON'T BE AFRAID TO LET GO OF THE NEGATIVE

Let's face it; there is a lot of negativity in this world. All you need to do is tune into the news or read the newspaper. And unfortunately, we are sometimes surrounded by negative people. Negative people and influences will weigh you down. Imagine an Olympic sprinter trying to run while dragging along a fifty-pound weight. He or she is not going to be able to achieve full potential until that weight is released. To achieve full potential in your career or life, you must let go of things that weigh you down. That might include associating with negative coworkers, friends, or even engaging in certain activities. We all know those people who always talk about how unhappy they are with their careers or their something going on in their personal lives and how they should make a change, but they are all talk and no action. These are the people you need to stay away from. In your life, strive to have only positive influences that will make a better you. Surround yourself with people who are winning in life or who have the desire to win.

This sign from Grant Cardone hangs in our office and shop.

CHAPTER 7

BE A FINISHER

You must always finish, period. You may not win, but by finishing, you are developing the mind-set of a winner. This will condition your mind to follow through in the future. Nobody wants to work with someone who can't finish the job. You want to have the reputation of someone who is dependable and can complete the task no matter what.

CHAPTER 8

SEEK OUT GREAT ADVICE

You have probably heard the saying that the most expensive advice is free advice. That often is the case. If you need advice on a matter, seek out those who are the leaders on that topic, and don't waste your time or effort on those who aren't or have little experience. Don't be afraid to pay for great advice. It can be an excellent investment.

CHAPTER 9

THE FINAL SCORE DOESN'T ALWAYS TELL WHO REALLY WON THE GAME

I n whatever you do, you should always give it your all, no matter what the score is. If you are seemingly running away with a victory, it is easy to get complacent and lose your edge. You may win this time, but the next time, you might get beat just because you aren't giving it 100 percent. If you didn't give it your all and weren't at your best, you might as well have lost—*lost* because you cheated yourself, not because of the outcome.

CHAPTER 10

KNOW EVERYTHING YOU CAN

F red Trump once said to his son Donald, "Know everything you can about what you are doing." You want every advantage you can get in business. Knowledge is one of the best advantages that you can have, especially if you have more knowledge than the competition does. Do your due diligence, and research all that there is to know about each deal or contract. You will be miles ahead of the other side, and it will show. A little homework will go a long way.

CHAPTER 11

CHALLENGE YOURSELF

To get better, you must challenge yourself to be better. It doesn't just happen on its own. Being competitive with yourself or others is a good trait to have. It keeps you on your toes. As long as you're green, you're growing. As soon as you're ripe, you start to rot. There is no standing still in business. Technology is constantly improving, and businesses are always searching for a better way to do things. New products are being invented every day. Do not become complacent. You always want to be striving to be at the top of your game. If a number-one professional sports team plays the worst team in the league all season and then goes into the championship game to play the number-two team, chances are they will find themselves face to face with defeat because they are not used to playing at a high level. Challenge yourself, and embrace competition.

CHAPTER 12

GET OUT OF YOUR COMFORT ZONE

You can't grow in your comfort zone. Nothing happens there. You grow muscle in the gym by damaging your muscles so they get larger. You expand your mind and your knowledge by learning and doing new things. I know it's hard. It's uncomfortable to put yourself out there, but that is simply how a person progresses.

Custom Tree Care's equipment fleet has grown a lot from its beginnings in 1999.

CHAPTER 13

DON'T STOP THREE FEET FROM GOLD

In the classic book *Think and Grow Rich,* Napoleon Hill tells a story about a man named R. U. Darby and his uncle who gave up on their dreams of becoming rich from gold mining because of temporary defeat. Though Darby had some setbacks, and he they quit digging, he was only three feet from a major gold vein. How do we know this? Because when he quit in frustration, he sold his digging machinery to a junk man for a few hundred dollars. The astute junk man called in a mining engineer who checked the mine and calculated that there was a vein of gold just three feet from where Darby had stopped digging. The junk man went on to make millions from the mine. Setbacks are a part of business and are to be expected. Don't ever let setbacks make you quit, because they are only temporary. Your greatest achievements could be just around the corner—you could be three feet from gold. If you give up, you will never reach it. Thomas Edison is said to have failed at inventing the light bulb ten thousand times. He never gave up, and he eventually succeeded. Henry Ford failed and went broke five times before he was successful. Where would we be in this world if everyone gave up when the going got tough? Failure can be a great teacher. Listen to it, learn from it, and move on. What you will learn from it can make you succeed the next time. R. H. Macy failed seven times before his store in New York City caught on. Failure is not permanent unless you quit. The past does not equal the future.

CHAPTER 14

CREATE TEAMS; TEAMS WIN GAMES AND DO THINGS

A single person cannot win a team game. Winning requires a team effort. Tom Brady is a great quarterback, but he can't win a game by himself. The same can be said for businesses. A business is made up of several moving parts working together for a common goal. If I have a crew on a tree-removal job, we may have one person doing the cutting. We will also have people on the ground assisting the cutter, cleaning up, and hauling away the debris. There is also someone who sold the job to the customer and someone in the office who will send out invoicing and keep the records. It's a team effort. Almost every business is set up the same way: the is management and there are the front lines in the field. They both need each other to do their jobs. An efficient team that works well together is hard to beat, no matter what you are doing.

CHAPTER 15

WORK WITH THE BEST

I f you work with the best, it will always pay off. If you are an employee, go work for the best company in your field because you will learn more. If you are in management, hire the best employees and have the best team because you will win more and be more profitable. Work with only the best contractors and use the best materials. Not only will that make your job easier, but also you will earn the reputation of being the best. When people have a choice, they will always choose the best because they know they will get something good. There is no substitute for high quality.

CHAPTER 16

If You're Going to Do It, Do It Right

If you are going to be doing a job anyway, why not do it right and do it big? Don't do it just to get by. No one likes mediocrity. I don't, my team doesn't, and I'm guessing you don't either. If you are not going to strive to win the race, why start? Play to win. Set yourself up to win beforehand by planning and preparing.

CHAPTER 17

Don't Make Excuses

Nobody likes excuses. They are a waste of time. That time should be spent on doing the job right and getting results. In today's information society, there are more resources available than ever before to help you succeed. Have the reputation of delivering results, not excuses. Always remember, you can't deposit excuses!

CHAPTER 18

TAKE SHOTS

Wayne Gretzky once said, "You miss one hundred percent of the shots you don't take." Simply put, you can't ever score and win if you don't take a shot. If you shoot, you might miss, but who cares? You might not miss, and you might even win a great victory. But if you don't take the shot, you already know the outcome. So, what are you waiting for? Take the shot. Take it right now.

CHAPTER 19

DON'T BE INSANE

Einstein defined insanity as "Doing the same thing over and over again and expecting different results." If something doesn't work, step back, analyze the problem, and see why the attempted solution failed. Then try again, and keep adjusting and trying until you succeed. Don't stab around blindly for an answer. That won't get you anywhere. See what worked before, and do it again. Improve on what didn't work well.

CHAPTER 20

BE PATIENT AND FOCUSED ON THE DESTINATION

S uccess rarely comes overnight. Those who do succeed usually are quite patient. You wouldn't plant an acorn one day and come back the next day and ask, "Why aren't you an oak tree yet?" People, projects, and businesses take time to grow and develop. Successful people also know that, to reach a goal, they must stay the course. When a plane takes off from the airport, it doesn't fly in straight line to its destination. The pilot adjusts the course several times around storms or other obstacles it encounters on the way. But the plane keeps moving with the end goal in mind.

CHAPTER 21

NEVER STOP LEARNING

When I was in school, I couldn't wait to be done. What I didn't realize was that I wasn't close to being done learning. I had hardly even begun to start learning. I mentioned earlier that the speed of business never slows, and neither should your learning. There are countless books, audio-books, DVDs, CDs, seminars, and magazines that can make you better. Reading a twenty-dollar book could help you make thousands, or even millions, of dollars.

I rarely fall asleep before 1:00 a.m., so late at night is a great time for me to read or listen to audiobooks on my iPhone. Maybe mornings work for you. If not, carve out another portion of your day. Get in a habit of spending some time on a regular basis to continue learning. Invest in yourself; it is the best investment you can make. Condition your mind for success, and visualize in your mind that you have already achieved success. Some of my favorite CD programs or audiobooks I routinely listen to while driving are from Tony Robbins, Grant Cardone, John Maxwell, and Robert Kiyosaki.

Always strive to be better than you were the day before in everything that you do. It doesn't have to be about business. It could be learning a new language or hobby, improving your marriage or other relationships, or becoming a better parent. Don't stop learning, ever!

CHAPTER 22

BE CONFIDENT

B e confident in everything that you do. Don't half-ass anything. I don't want to work with people who aren't confident in their abilities, and you shouldn't either. Don't be cocky by any means, but when you speak, do so with the attitude that you know what you are talking about and can back it up. When you are selling, the consumers aren't just buying a product or service; they are buying value from you. They sure won't buy if they aren't confident you will deliver as promised.

Confidence will get you more work, more contacts, and more money. Your employees or coworkers will trust you more and work harder as well, because you are a leader. First impressions mean a lot. Have a firm handshake and make eye contact when you meet someone. Also make eye contact when someone is speaking to you. Remember the person's name, ask for his or her contact information, and make sure to follow up.

Confidence comes from doing. Even if you are a little unsure of yourself, don't let it show. Most of the time, no one will know the difference. Just make sure you back up what you say. Be confident enough that you make people believe they would be crazy not to work with you.

CHAPTER 23

BE SMART

Everyone makes mistakes. I have, and I will make a lot more, and that's okay. That's part of learning. Learn from your mistakes and the mistakes of others, and don't repeat them. Make good decisions. There are more resources available today on every topic imaginable. There is no excuse for not making an informed decision. If you're inexperienced in a certain area, talk to someone who is an expert. Or better yet, talk to everyone you can who is an expert. Do your homework, and make a smart decision. That's smart.

CHAPTER 24

CRUSH THE COMPETITION

Business is a game, just like sports. There are winners and losers, number ones and number twos. Always strive to be the best; always strive to be number one. Always operate with integrity, and have respect for your competitors as they help move your industry and the economy forward. But have the mind-set that every dollar they make is one you or your company should or could have made. If I lose a contract or a deal, I see it as money out of my company's and my family's hands. I hate losing money to the competition, but I don't worry about them. We crush them by doing what we do far better than they do and doing more of it.

CHAPTER 25

LEVERAGE

This is one of my favorite words. *Leverage* simply means doing more with less effort. I was and still am a great tree cutter. But there are only so many trees you can cut in a day and a limit to what you can reasonably charge a customer for each tree. So, I decided to manage several people cutting trees. I still worked the same number of hours or fewer, but we were getting ten times as much done. That is the only way you can grow.

CHAPTER 26

ENLIST EXPERTS

Business can be complex, with a daunting number of laws and regulations to follow in several areas. Take a deep breath; you don't have to know everything about everything to be a great owner or manager. However, you should know what person to turn to when you need answers quickly. This person could be an accountant, attorney, financial advisor, banker, or consultant. One person couldn't possibly be an expert in all these areas. You wouldn't schedule a visit with your dentist to solve a problem with your foot, would you? It doesn't make any more sense for you to decide on something yourself regarding an area you know very little about.

You should be consulting with experts on a regular basis to review your operations and make sure you are on the right track. Doing so may save you a headache down the road by catching a problem early and correcting it quickly. Business owners sometimes try to do everything on their own, thinking that no one else can do it right. If you have that attitude, you will never achieve the success you are capable of.

CHAPTER 27

TAKE ACTION

There are times when a great opportunity presents itself. You should be able to recognize and evaluate these moments and act quickly. If you sit back and wait, that opportunity may not come around again. If it's a good move for you personally or professionally, then go for it. Don't waste time. Time is the most valuable thing on this planet. You can't buy it, and you can't get it back, so don't waste it by waiting. Nike has the greatest marketing slogan of all time, "Just do it."

One of the biggest detriments to success is delaying action or, even worse, not acting at all. Assemble as much information about whatever it is you need to decide on, look at all the possible outcomes, weigh the pros and cons of each, make the best decision, and stick with it. Many deals are lost due to inaction. Not taking action or making a decision is an action; it can't move you forward in almost all cases, however. The most successful people take action quickly. Do more than the competition, and do it quicker. Just do it.

CHAPTER 28

PROMOTE YOURSELF

You are your own brand. Always promote yourself by making sure people know who you are and what you do. Never miss an opportunity to grow your business. Every contact you make could turn out to be a great client and a source of revenue. Make sure you always have business cards with you wherever you go. If you drive a company vehicle, have the company name, logo, and website or phone number on the door. Or better yet, have it on all sides. If you are out and about, wear a nice company shirt. People will notice you. Promote yourself in everything that you do.

Accepting the Inc. 500 award in Washington D.C. in 2009.

CHAPTER 29

KNOW THAT YOU CAN'T FIX EVERYTHING

I am all for making things work and driving on to reach a goal even when the odds are stacked against me. But sometimes you and I must know when to lose a battle to win the war. There are things you cannot control and people you will deal with who simply cannot be persuaded nor reasoned with. Move on from those things and people, and focus on what you can control.

CHAPTER 30

KEEP EXCELLENT RECORDS

I t is necessary to keep accurate and complete records for many reasons, however a lot of businesses fail to do so. Good records will help you track income, deduct expenses, and provide data for you to analyze. You need accurate data to generate reports such as a balance sheet, income statement, profit and loss statement, and tax return. In the event of an IRS audit, you need to provide records of legitimate business expenses. If you are in retail, you need to have a solid inventory system to know how much you are selling and how much of a certain product you have on hand. Every business should maintain a database with all past clients' contact names, addresses, phone numbers, e-mails, and transaction histories. I was once looking at buying an existing business, and I asked the owner if he had a client list. He replied that he just wrote their names in a spiral notebook when they paid. The value of that business went down greatly in my eyes because we didn't even have a way to contact past customers. I did not purchase that business.

It is also wise to backup your data in another secure location in case your computer system crashes or there is a natural disaster where your records are destroyed. Keep excellent records—your accountant will appreciate it as well.

CHAPTER 31

ACT BIGGER THAN YOU ARE

Acting bigger than you are is like confidence; it will get you more jobs. When you speak to someone about a major project, act as if you have done jobs that big or that complex before. I am not suggesting that you be dishonest by any means or act arrogant. However, you should stress that you can get the job done and have the resources to do so properly. When you market yourself and your company, let the public know you can handle anything. Look professional, act as if you've been there before, and look like a big company, even if you're not. You are going to be one, someday very soon.

CHAPTER 32

SET GOALS, AND HAVE A PLAN

If you want success, you must know what you want. Set goals for everything you do. The clearer your goals and your plan to achieve them, the better your chances of success. An army doesn't go into battle without a battle plan and the objective of defeating the enemy. Your success is no different. Write your goals down, and review them daily. Tell everyone what the goals are. This puts more pressure on you to achieve them. Set big goals, and stay focused on them. Things will come up, and you will need to adjust your plan at times. Don't ever lose sight of where you are going, though.

CHAPTER 33

COMMIT, AND THINK LONG TERM

For the most part, there are no overnight successes. The people at the top didn't wake up and just get there by chance. They have an unwavering level of commitment to whatever they are involved in and are in it for the long haul. They didn't give up when they met difficulties.

CHAPTER 34

HAVE AN OPEN MIND

When analyzing a deal—no matter what kind of deal it is—look at it thoroughly with an open mind. Do not let what happened in the past blind you to what is possible. The past does not equal the future. Run the ramifications of each scenario through your head. Or better yet, discuss it with your team members to get their input. What is the best thing that can happen for each course of action? What is the worst thing that can happen? Use logic and facts, and make an informed decision.

CHAPTER 35

GIVE BACK

The act of giving to another is one of the most rewarding things a human being can do. A person does not have to be super successful to give—or even successful at all. The more success you have, however, the greater the impact you can have. If you don't have a great deal of money, you can donate your time. My wife and I donate money both personally and through our companies to several great charities in our area. We also donate our time by delivering food through Harvesters, a great organization to help feed America's hungry, and by serving food at the Topeka Rescue Mission through Forge, a group of young professionals in Topeka. Giving helps others in need and will improve the community that you live and do business in. Give, give, give, and it will come back to you.

My wife Maura is an amazing person and a great partner in all that we do.

CHAPTER 36

FIND OUT WHAT YOU'RE GOOD AT AND WHAT YOU'RE NOT GOOD AT

I am good at a lot of things. I will also admit that there are a lot of things I am not good at. Someone successful does not need to be good at everything.

I don't care who you are. You should delegate the things you are not good at to those that are. This allows you to maximize your effectiveness. I see so many small business owners who are great at a skilled trade and go into business, only to go out of business shortly thereafter. Or they never grow the business because they try to do everything by themselves and can't manage. That is an insane and failing formula.

CHAPTER 37

PROTECT YOURSELF

Unfortunately, bad things happen in this world every day. For the most part, many of these are out of our control. It is your responsibility to protect yourself, your business, and your family from risk. Minimize that risk as much as possible. You are required to have insurance on your home, business, and car in case of a loss. Most people also should have—although many don't—decent health insurance and life insurance. In my opinion, term life is the best choice because you can get a lot more coverage for less money compared to whole life. If you then invest the difference you saved by purchasing term life versus whole life, you will ultimately add to your net worth.

It is also a good idea to have insurance on key people in your organization in the event of a death. I learned that lesson the hard way when I lost my director of operations unexpectedly to a massive heart attack. Also, you should have a rock-solid noncompete agreement with key employees. Another way to protect yourself is to make sure your business is set up properly from a legal standpoint. I would suggest meeting with an attorney who specializes in business law. Make sure your company name, logos, and products are trademarked or copyrighted. In not protecting yourself you are vulnerable to lawsuits, in which case, even if you win, you will be set back by the expenses to defend your case. One mistake or accident can take away everything you have. Don't let that happen to you and your people.

CHAPTER 38

SEE THE BIG PICTURE

Keep your focus on where you are going and why you are doing it. Don't let things distract you from your goals. Make sure the details are handled, but at the same time, always have an awareness of the big picture. Remember where you are going, not where you are or where you were.

CHAPTER 39

HAVE YOUR MONEY WORK FOR YOU

You will never get rich working for money. Even if you have a high-paying job, you can do only so much, and there are only so many hours in a day. I was a great tree trimmer when I started my tree-care business, but I could only trim so many trees in one day. The highest paid heart surgeon in the United States can only perform so many operations. And if that heart surgeon stops performing operations, guess what happens to his revenue. It stops as well.

Don't get me wrong; we need heart surgeons and tree trimmers. What I am saying is no matter how much you make, you need to invest and have money work for you. Start today, and get in the habit of setting aside a portion of your income. Invest in something that will provide a good return. It can be a business you start, the stock market, a retirement account, or (my personal preference) rental real estate. The earlier in life you start investing, the better off you are. Make it an expense that you pay first every month no matter what. Don't do it with whatever is left over. Make money while you sleep, not just when you are on the clock.

CHAPTER 40

REMEMBER THAT CASH FLOW IS KING

The lifeblood of any operation, business or personal, is cash. Cold, hard cash. You want it, and you need it. Don't take this as me sounding greedy. I am trying to stress the importance of this. It's what pays your house payment, the food for your family, the things you need to survive in society, and hopefully whatever extra you want to do as well. It is also a means in which you can give back to your community and help others.

Cash flow is simple to understand. All you need to do is make more than you spend so that you have a surplus and not a deficit. If I receive $1,500 a month gross income from a property and my expenses are $1,000 a month, I generate $500 a month positive monthly cash flow from just that one property. If I own ten properties producing that same cash flow, that translates into $60,000 a year passive. What if you own one hundred units—or one thousand? That's $600,000 and $6,000,000 positive cash flow respectively. Now that's some serious cash. Can you use an extra $60,000 a year? How about $6,000,000? What could you do for your family and community if you had that kind of cash flow?

Robert Kiyosaki designed two games called CashFlow and CashFlow for Kids. We have them in our house, and they're a great way to understand this concept and have a little fun as well. Your objective is to get out of the rat race by getting your passive income greater than your expenses.

This is a great game to teach kids how money can work for you.

CHAPTER 41

HAVE AN EMERGENCY FUND

Just as it is imperative that you invest a certain portion of your income, it is just as important to save some of it. Put savings in your expense column automatically. Look, unexpected stuff happens: people get sick or hurt, or they lose their jobs. Your expenses aren't going to stop. Maybe your refrigerator goes out, and you need to replace it right away. Be prepared so if your income stops, you have a cushion and can handle it.

CHAPTER 42

DON'T BE AFRAID TO SEEK EXPERT ADVICE, IF YOU MUST

I strongly dislike having to use attorneys for anything unless it's really needed. They can be expensive, and litigation can drag on for months or even years. However, there are many times you must use a lawyer to either protect yourself or your business, to go after money that is owed to you, or to help draw up or review legal documents. Some people and some businesses are out to take advantage of you and bury you at any cost. You can't let that happen or get the reputation that you can be walked all over. Sometimes a properly filed lawsuit can be the best thing to do. There are many different attorneys who specialize in different aspects of law. My advice is to find the one who will give you the best service and quickest results for whatever you need. Avoid it if you can; if not, hit your adversaries hard.

Think back to Napoleon Hill's story of R.U. Darby who had stopped digging three feet from a major gold vein. Had the junk man to whom he sold the digging machinery not sought the expert advice of the mining engineer, he would not have known that Darby's project had failed merely because they were not familiar with fault lines, and that, after a little calculating, the vein could be found just three feet from where Darby had stopped digging. The junk man ended up taking millions of dollars in gold from Darby's former mine because he was smart enough to know what he didn't know, and he sought expert counsel before giving up.

CHAPTER 43

WORK ON, NOT IN

Change your mind-set from working *in* your business to working *on* your business. You can't really grow if you are the one doing the actual work in the field. When I made this change in my tree service in 2005, our revenues increased from about $200,000 annually to more than $2,000,000 annually in just three years. If you are a business owner not focused on working on the business, all you will ever have is a job working in the business.

My growth accelerated once I stopped working in the business and started working on the business.

CHAPTER 44

BE A GOOD COMMUNICATOR

The most important skill in business is communication. It is probably the most important skill in life, period. You need to be able to convey your thoughts, wants, needs, and objectives to others. How can you lead your team members if you can't communicate what they need to do? Would you expect clients to buy from you if you could not describe to them what the product or service will do for them and what value it holds? If you cannot, it will be very difficult to make a single sale.

All people are in sales, whether they realize it or not and regardless of what their titles are. Everyone is selling something all the time, be it ideas, products, services, real estate, an agenda, or oneself. It is your job to convince and persuade somebody to do what you want and close the deal. You don't close the deal unless you communicate clearly and to the point. And you don't get the result you want until you close the deal.

There are entire books written on this subject, and I'm not here to cover all the details. I urge you to continually train yourself in communication. People communicate with other people not just by talking to one another but also through e-mail, texts, letters, and advertisements. A person's nonverbal communication often means more than words alone. Believe me, my wife can give me a look, and I know exactly what she means without her uttering a single word!

CHAPTER 45

STRIVE TO BE RICH

It should be your goal to be rich—not just rich in money, but rich in life. Money is not everything and should not be the most important thing you strive for, but if you are on planet earth and breathing, you need it. It costs a lot to survive. And you shouldn't want to just survive. Thrive!!!

A lot of money can help you achieve a lot of things, a lot of great things. You can do more when you're rich. You can do more for others. You can give more. You can provide better for yourself, your friends, and your family if you are rich. The Bill and Melinda Gates Foundation donated $50 million to help end the recent Ebola outbreak in West Africa. I think their ability to give like that is amazing, and I commend them. Do you think they could do that if they were not rich?

I like to buy the highest quality products and services I can. I'd rather fly in a private jet than a commercial plane. I'd rather drive a Mercedes Benz than a Kia. I want to go on a lot of vacations with my family and show them the world. I'd rather stay at a Four Seasons than a Motel Six. I want to have a big retirement account saved up. I want to have money in the bank in case something bad happens. And I want to send my kids to the best schools and the best doctors. All that costs money and a lot of it. So, I'd rather be rich, and so should you. Striving to be rich makes you push your-self to reach your potential and goals.

CHAPTER 46

HIRE SLOW, FIRE FAST

Organizations are made up of people. Great organizations are made up of great people moving toward a common goal. So don't waste your time or tolerate a substandard work ethic. If someone isn't doing the work as they should, work with them to improve, but if they won't, get rid of them and fast! Bad employees are like cancer and can pollute your entire team. They may steal from you, bring down morale, hamper production, and cost you money. Stop the bleeding. Once the decision is made to remove them, do not wait.

When hiring, do your homework and don't get in a hurry. I don't care a whole lot about college degrees or résumés. What counts is what the applicant has done, how they work with others, and what they can do for the organization. Attitude trumps skill every time. You can train skill. However, it is almost impossible to correct a bad attitude. Take your time interviewing someone, ask the right questions, and do your homework to see if he or she is the right person. So, hire slow and fire fast.

CHAPTER 47

REMEMBER THAT WE ALL HAVE THE SAME POTENTIAL

Every person on this planet has the same 365 days in a year and 24 hours in a day. It's what you do with that time that determines your success. If you want life to be better, you must be better.

CHAPTER 48

Use Systems

The best and most successful businesses are the ones with the best system, not the best products. Think of most fast-food chains. Most people can cook a better hamburger than McDonalds, but there are McDonalds restaurants around the world. McDonalds has an amazing system for operating a fast-food restaurant and is the most successful franchise of all time. It's the playbook of how to do what you do efficiently. Having a system lets you leverage and replicate your business anywhere.

CHAPTER 49

HAVE PASSION

Passion is by far the most important trait that an entrepreneur must have to be successful. It's the "why" in the "why you do what you do." Passion is inside you. It's what keeps you going when everything is against you. When most people would stop and quit, your passion keeps you going. Every time you get knocked down, passion gets you up again and again until you achieve your goal.

CHAPTER 50

DO WHAT YOUR COMPETITION WON'T

The greatest thing you can do to set yourself apart from your competition is to do what they won't do. You can have the same product or service as a competitor, but maybe you can deliver it better, offer better service, have better hours, market or advertise differently, or have better locations. The only thing you can control is your effort.

CHAPTER 51

HAVE THE RIGHT ATTITUDE

Keep in mind the wise words of Charles R. Swindoll, "Life is 10% what happens to you and 90% how you react to it." I cannot stress how important the right attitude is to your success. Life is hard, and there will be problems. The only way to not have problems is to not be living.

Look forward to problems. That sounds crazy, I know. But problems are merely opportunities. The more problems you solve, the stronger you become and the more people you help. The more people you help, the more success you will have.

CHAPTER 52

EXERCISE AND EAT HEALTHFULLY

God gave you only one body. It's like a machine. Take care of it, and you will maximize your life. Don't take care of it, and you will have an increased risk of disease and health problems, both of which can lead to an early death. It's a little hard to be successful when you're sick, or worse, dead.

You will be more productive when your body is in top operating condition. You will have more energy to do the things you want or need to do. Eat things that are good for you. Don't eat fast food or junk food. Why do you think it's called *junk* food? Work out regularly. You don't need to be a power lifter or a marathon runner, but be active and do something to raise your heart rate and build strength. Start out easy and slowly work your way up. I hate getting up early, but it's best if you work out in the morning and get moving. It will set the tone for the day, and you will accomplish much more.

CHAPTER 53

REMEMBER PARETO'S PRINCIPLE

One of the greatest things I have ever learned is Pareto's Principle: 80 percent of your results will come from 20 percent of your efforts. Basically, this is saying to focus on the things that are most productive and get you the most results. About 80 percent of your revenue is probably coming from the top 20 percent of your clients. Delegate the rest, or maybe don't deal with them at all.

CHAPTER 54

FOCUS WELL; YOU GO WHERE YOU FOCUS

One of the not-so-bright things I did when I was in high school was riding bulls. I decided that there wasn't much of a future in riding bulls even if you were very good, so I didn't stick with it long. But I do remember that they taught me that wherever I looked, that's where I would naturally go. They taught me to tuck my chin and look straight down at the bull's shoulders. If I looked at the ground, that's where I would go, and it wasn't a soft landing either. The same can be said about business and goals. Focus on where you need to be, and don't be so distracted by the other things going on that can throw you into the dirt if you take your eyes off the bull.

You will gravitate to what you focus on.

CHAPTER 55

TAKE CHARGE, AND TAKE RESPONSIBILITY

Leaders need to take charge of their teams. Great leaders take ownership of everything, no matter what. If you're the CEO, you are ultimately responsible for what happens. Don't pass the buck or blame others. That's what weak people do. And weak people will never be successful.

CHAPTER 56

HAVE MULTIPLE INCOME STREAMS

You've probably heard the saying "Don't have all your eggs in one basket." The same rings true for income. Most millionaires derive their income from multiple sources. Stocks, real estate, businesses, and other investments are just a few, in addition to a career. If one source is impacted by a downturn, you will have the others to fall back on. There is no shortage of ways to make money in this country, and there is no excuse why you shouldn't have your own multiple ways.

CHAPTER 57

Operate at High Levels

I don't care what you do or what business or industry you're in—you're going to have to take massive amounts of action if you're going to be successful. In life, in business, in relationships, there is only one way to operate, and that is at high levels. Nothing else will produce results, and nothing else pays. So get out there, and raise your level.

CHAPTER 58

FIND MENTORS

If you want to be successful, you can save a lot of time by studying those individuals and organizations that have been successful already. Do what they do and did. Learn what worked for them and what didn't work for them. Learn from their mistakes. Get your hands on anything that you can about success, and study it nonstop.

The following is a list of notable leaders whom I have studied and learned from. I've read their books, studied them, listened to them on YouTube, and gone through their self-help programs. It's not an all-inclusive list, but I encourage you to do the same and watch your knowledge expand.

- Grant Cardone—author, motivational speaker, real estate investor, and expert in growth and sales training
- Tony Robbins—motivational speaker, author, businessman, and expert in human behavior, wellness, and relationships
- John Maxwell—author, speaker, pastor, and expert in leadership
- Napoleon Hill—author well known for improving the self for success

- Marty Grunder—businessman, speaker, author, and consultant
- Dale Carnegie—author and developer of famous courses in self-improvement, speaking, and interpersonal skills
- Jim Rohn—entrepreneur, author, and motivational speaker
- Robert Kiyosaki—author and developer of several products to increase one's financial independence
- Zig Ziglar—author, salesman, and motivational speaker
- Steve Jobs—businessman and inventor
- Les Brown—motivational speaker
- Greg Plitt—fitness model, speaker, and authority on nutrition, motivation, and exercise
- Donald Trump—forty-fifth and current president of the United States; successful businessman, author, and TV personality
- Tom Hopkins—creator of several products for sales training
- Eric Thomas—motivational speaker, author, and minister
- Ray Kroc—businessman who built McDonalds into the most successful fast-food operation in the world

Author Biography

G reg Gathers graduated from Kansas State University. His company made the Inc. 500 list in 2009, the Inc. 5000 list in 2016 and 2017, and the 2017 Ingram's Corporate Report 100. It was honored by the KSBDC with the 2009 Existing Small Business of the Year Award. It also won the 2012 National Award from Keep America Beautiful.

Gathers was a graduate of Leadership Topeka in 2013 and was named a 20 Under 40 honoree in 2011. He started his business from nothing and is now living proof that with the right amount of determination, anyone can rise above their circumstances and achieve uncommon success. He resides in Topeka, Kansas with his wife and children.

www.ingramcontent.com/pod-product-compliance
Lightning Source LLC
Chambersburg PA
CBHW061201180526
45170CB00002B/906